COELOPHYSIS

by Janet Riehecky
illustrated by Lydia Halverson

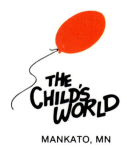

THE CHILD'S WORLD

MANKATO, MN

Grateful appreciation is expressed to
Bret S. Beall, Research Consultant,
Field Museum of Natural History, Chicago,
Illinois, who reviewed this book to
insure its accuracy.

Library of Congress Cataloging in Publication Data

Riehecky, Janet, 1953-
  Coelophysis / by Janet Riehecky ; illustrated by Lydia Halverson.
    p. cm. — (Dinosaur books)
  Summary: Describes what is known and hypothesized about the
physical appearance and behavior of the small carnivorous dinosaur
called Coelophysis.
  ISBN 0-89565-623-X (lib. bdg.)
  1. Coelophysis—Juvenile literature. [1. Coelophysis.
2. Dinosaurs.] I. Halverson, Lydia, ill. II. Title. III. Series:
Riehecky, Janet, 1953-   Dinosaur books.
QE862.S3R533   1990
567.9'7—dc20   90-38273
                                   CIP
                                   AC

COELOPHYSIS

Two hundred million years ago, the world was much different from what it is today. No grass grew. No flowers bloomed.

It was a hotter world than today's. And
the animals were mostly reptiles.

Strange flying reptiles soared
through the skies.

Other weird reptiles swam in the seas.

On land there were some familar reptiles, such as crocodiles, turtles, and
lizards . . .

and also some of the most unusual reptiles
that ever lived—the dinosaurs!

At first the dinosaurs were just another group of animals, but before too long, they became the rulers of their world—and they stayed on top for one hundred and forty million years!

One of the very first dinosaurs to appear on earth was a small meat eater called Coelophysis (see-lo-FI-sis). It was a small, lightly-built dinosaur, but it was a successful hunter. Its descendants lived throughout the age of dinosaurs.

Scientists have known for many years that one of the first dinosaurs was Coelophysis, but they didn't know much about it until 1947. In 1947 several scientists, who were on their way to the Petrified Forest National Monument, stopped for a few days at Ghost Ranch, Arizona. They

searched in rock dating from the very be-
ginning of the dinosaur age. One found
some pieces of a dinosaur's backbone, leg,
and claw.

Eventually over one hundred skeletons of Coelophysis were found at Ghost Ranch. They showed that the Coelophysis was quite small compared to the dinosaurs that came after it, though it wasn't small compared to people. It stretched eight to ten feet from the tip of its tail to the end of its nose. Its hips were three or four feet from the ground. It was tall enough to look a person in the eye, but most of the later dinosaurs would have towered over it.

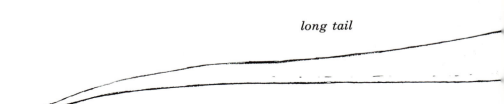

long tail

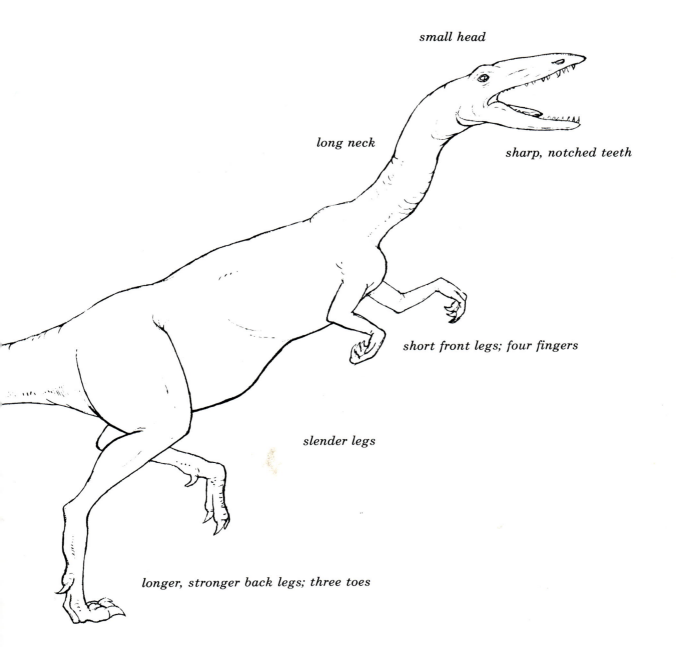

small head

long neck

sharp, notched teeth

short front legs; four fingers

slender legs

longer, stronger back legs; three toes

15

Despite the fact that the Coelophysis was as big as many people, it weighed less than a hundred pounds. That's because its body was very slender, and its length was mostly tail and neck. Also, many of its bones were hollow. In fact, the name Coelophysis means ''hollow form.''

Like the other meat-eating dinosaurs that lived later, the Coelophysis ran on its two back legs, saving its shorter front legs to use as arms—for grabbing its next meal. Its hands had three fingers with claws and one very short finger. The Coelophysis was good at grabbing and

holding onto such things as frogs. (Even two hundred million years ago, frogs' legs were a popular meal.)

The Coelophysis was a good hunter. It had large eyes and small, sharp teeth. It ran swiftly, leaving little, birdlike footprints behind.

The Coelophysis probably hunted small animals most of the time: tiny mammals, frogs, and even an occasional scorpion. It probably also enjoyed various insects: ants, termites, cockroaches, and dragonflies. (And they weren't even chocolate coated!) These small animals could move swiftly, but the Coelophysis moved even faster!

Some scientists think that packs of these swift hunters worked together to hunt big animals. A large pack could attack an animal that was bigger than the entire pack and still win.

But because one Coelophysis was pretty
small by itself, a Coelophysis that strayed
from the pack may have sometimes ended
up as the dinner instead of the diner.

There were huge crocodile-like creatures named Phytosaurs (FI-toe-sawrs) that lived at the same time. If a Phytosaur caught a Coelophysis by itself, it was, "See you later, Coelophysis!"

The Phytosaurs stayed near the rivers most of the time, so the Coelophysis dinosaurs probably spent most of their time in the drier, upland woods. Scientists think they roamed the woods in packs, looking for food and trying to stay out of trouble.

As the years passed, the earth changed a lot. Plants grew to huge sizes. Many more dinosaurs appeared, and many of them also grew to huge sizes. But small dinosaurs like Coelophysis did not disappear.

During all the millions of years of the dinosaur age, the earth continued to change. Flowers and modern plants appeared. Strange new dinosaurs appeared.

But there were still little meat-eating dinosaurs, related to Coelophysis, successfully hunting small animals and trying to stay out of the way of the bigger meat eaters.

 # Dinosaur Fun

You may think that the world of the dinosaurs was completely different from the world of today, but that's not true. Some kinds of animals that were around when dinosaurs were alive are still around today!

Many reptiles, such as lizards, snakes, turtles, and tortoises, were alive during the age of dinosaurs. Even frogs and toads lived alongside dinosaurs. So did many insects, such as dragonflies, cockroaches, and butterflies. But the closest living relatives of dinosaurs are crocodiles and, many scientists believe, birds.

Look through magazines and newspapers for pictures of the animals named above. Clip them out and paste them to a piece of poster board. Or you can draw pictures of these animals. Label your poster, "Animals from the Age of Dinosaurs."